This book belongs to

....

PARTY TIME!

CONTENTS

Hi. We're The Wiggles, and we LOVE birthday parties. Some might even consider us experts in this area! So we're here to help you plan the best birthday party ever for your little Wiggle.

Fruit Salad TV

Do you remember the **WIGGLES OF ANTICIPATION** you felt as a child as it grew closer and closer to your birthday?

Do you remember planning your birthday party, getting **MORE AND MORE EXCITED** about all the possibilities for your special day?

Well, we're happy to tell you that some things never change. Children today still have the same wishes, wants and dreams for their birthday parties. And as their party planner, throwing them the **BIRTHDAY BASH OF THEIR DREAMS** can be as simple as singing 'Happy birthday to you'. You just need a few special ingredients and you'll be hosting the Wiggliest birthday party ever.

THE BIG DAY JUST TAKES A LITTLE IMAGINATION AND ORGANISATION.

First, decide on the theme of the party, then build the food (and fun) around this. For our Tea Party, we've got little sandwiches and teacup trifles. For our Little Chefs party, you'll find gourmet pizzas and waffles. A Pyjama Party wouldn't be the same without popcorn and hot chocolate. In Under the Sea, it's fish tacos and sea rocks, while partygoers at our Animal Party will eat Goofy Hot Dogs and Bee Sushi. For drinks, we've created exciting flavours for milkshakes, smoothies, slushies, lemonade and hot chocolate for kids to slurp through. Yum!

We haven't forgotten the all-important birthday cake, of course. Dorothy loves tea so we've included a Teapot cake, and you'll also find a couple of favourite Wiggles characters in cakes too: Henry the Octopus and Wags the Dog. And you can never go wrong with a Wiggly Rainbow cake or a multi-coloured Wiggles Keyboard cake. Because we all need more music, singing and dancing in our lives, don't we?

We've even included ideas for the take-home goody bags. No Wiggle will leave your party empty-handed!

INGREDIENTS FOR A WIGGLY PARTY

- ☐ CHOOSE A THEME
- ☐ INVITATIONS
- ☐ ACTIVITIES & ENTERTAINMENT
- ☐ MUSIC
- ☐ YUMMY FOOD
- ☐ BIRTHDAY CAKE
- ☐ GOODY BAGS

Now, it's time to **GET YOUR WIGGLE ON** and host the **WIGGLIEST BIRTHDAY PARTY EVER!**

The Wiggles
John, Evie, Tsehay, Lachy, Simon, Anthony and Kelly

TEA
PARTY

You're invited to _____ [name] birthday tea party,
in celebration of them turning _____ [age] !

WHEN

On a lovely
sunny day

TIME

Tea time

WHERE

In a country
garden

DRESS UP

In your
prettiest clothes

PLEASE BRING

Lots of smiles
& laughter

PREP + COOK TIME
UNDER
30 MINS

BOW SCONES

**350g butternut pumpkin, chopped
into 2cm pieces**
2 tbsp milk, plus extra for brushing
**1½ cups self-raising flour,
plus extra for dusting**
1 tsp baking powder
50g cold butter, chopped
1 cup grated cheddar cheese
6 cherry tomatoes, halved
250g spreadable cream cheese

Preheat oven to 200°C. Grease a large oven tray; line with baking paper.

Place pumpkin and 2 tablespoons water in a microwave-safe bowl; microwave on HIGH (100%) for 5 minutes or until tender. Drain well. Return to bowl with milk; use a fork to mash until smooth. Set aside to cool slightly.

Meanwhile, sift flour and baking powder into a bowl; rub in butter with your fingertips until it resembles fine crumbs. Stir in cheese and pumpkin mixture. Using a dinner knife, cut wet ingredients through flour mixture to form a soft, sticky dough.

Gently knead dough on a floured surface until smooth, then pat out until 2.5cm thick. Using a floured 10cm bow-shaped cutter, cut out as many bow shapes as possible. Press scraps together and repeat patting and cutting to make 12 bows in total. Place bows on tray; brush tops with extra milk. Bake for 12 minutes or until golden. Cool on tray.

Top each bow with a cherry tomato half, cut-side down, securing with a little cream cheese. Cut bows in half horizontally, spread bases with remaining cream cheese, then sandwich together with bow tops.

WIGGLY TIP
Scones are best
eaten on the day of
making or freeze,
undecorated, for
up to 1 month.

PREP + COOK TIME
UNDER 15 MINS

MAKES 14 WIGGLY SANDWICHES

SANDWICH SHAPES

28 slices wholemeal bread
½ cup Greek-style spreadable
  cream cheese
200g baby cherry tomatoes,
  sliced thinly

Using an 11cm star-shaped cutter, cut stars from each slice of bread, then using a 5cm star-shaped cutter, cut out a smaller star from the centre of half the stars (see Wiggly tips).

Spread one side of the larger uncut stars with 2 teaspoons cream cheese, then top with cherry tomato slices, overlapping them slightly. Spread the remaining cream cheese on one side of the larger cut stars, then place on top of the tomato, cheese-side down (see Wiggly tips).

Wiggly tips Why not use your favourite shaped cutter instead. We've used star-, heart-, flower- and teddy-shaped cutters. The little star cut-outs can be used to make fairy bread.

Prep it Sandwiches can be made 3 hours ahead and stored, covered, in the fridge.

MAKES 20 WIGGLY BLINIS

BUTTERFLY BLINIS

1 small avocado

2 tsp lemon juice

5 baby orange grape tomatoes
(see Wiggly tip)

¼ cup (65g) beetroot dip

65g cream cheese, at room
temperature

20 mini blinis (168g)

10 pretzel sticks, cut into 2cm lengths

Cut avocado in half lengthways; remove seed then peel. Cut each half lengthways again to make four wedges, then cut 40 small triangles from avocado wedges; drizzle with lemon juice (this will stop the avocado from turning brown).

Cut each grape tomato lengthways into quarters.

Combine beetroot dip and cream cheese in a small bowl.

Spread each blini with 1 heaped teaspoon of beetroot mixture. Using the picture as a guide, arrange avocado triangles on beetroot mixture for the wings and position pretzel sticks for the antennae; place a tomato quarter on top for the body.

Wiggly tip Baby orange grape tomatoes can be found in punnets of Mix A Mato tomatoes, available at major supermarkets and greengrocers.

PREP IT
Beetroot dip mixture can be made a day ahead and stored, covered, in the fridge.

WIGGLY TIP
To achieve the perfect jelly cube, set jelly in a takeaway container.

PREP + COOK TIME

UNDER
15 MINS
+ OVERNIGHT
REFRIGERATION

MAKES 12 WIGGLY TRIFLES

TEACUP TRIFLES

2 x 85g packets strawberry
 jelly crystals
2 cups (500ml) boiling water
2 baby mandarins
125g madeira cake, cut into
 1cm cubes
125g raspberries
125g small strawberries, quartered
½ cup thick and creamy
 vanilla yoghurt
½ cup passionfruit curd
ready-made sugar flowers, butterflies,
 hearts and sprinkles, to decorate

Place jelly crystals in a heatproof bowl and add the water; stir until crystals dissolve. Cool slightly. Pour jelly mixture into an 11cm x 17cm sealable container (see Wiggly tip); seal. Refrigerate overnight or until firm.

Once set, turn jelly out onto a board; cut into 1cm cubes. Refrigerate until needed.

Peel and segment mandarins.

Divide cake, jelly cubes, mandarin segments, raspberries and strawberries between 12 x ¾-cup teacups, jars or paper cups. Spoon over yoghurt and curd. Decorate each trifle with sugar flowers, butterflies, hearts and sprinkles.

Prep it Teacup trifles are best assembled close to serving.

TEDDY BEAR
ROLLS

MAKES 20 WIGGLY SAUSAGE ROLLS

TEDDY BEAR ROLLS

500g pork and veal mince
1 medium apple, grated finely
1 medium carrot, grated finely
1 small onion, grated coarsely
⅓ cup coarse breadcrumbs
1 tbsp barbecue sauce, plus extra
  to decorate
2 tsp chopped sage leaves
2 sheets puff pastry, thawed
1 egg, beaten lightly
tomato sauce, to serve

Preheat oven to 200°C. Grease two large oven trays; line with baking paper.

Place mince, apple, carrot, onion, breadcrumbs, barbecue sauce and sage in a large bowl; mix well.

Divide mince mixture in half. Working with one half at a time, divide into three equal portions. Combine two portions together; shape into a 3cm x 24cm log. Divide remaining portion into two; shape each into a thinner 24cm long log. Repeat with remaining mince mixture.

Place a large log along the edge of one pastry sheet, leaving a 2cm border (step 1). Roll pastry border over log to just enclose. Place one thinner log on pastry sheet next to the enclosed log (step 2), then roll enclosed log over thin log once. Place the second thinner log on pastry sheet next to enclosed logs, then roll enclosed logs over to the end of pastry sheet. Brush edge with a little egg and press to seal. Refrigerate for 30 minutes or until firm. Repeat with remaining logs and pastry sheet to make two rolls. Using your hands, gently press along each ear line to form bear-shaped rolls (step 3). Refrigerate for 30 minutes or until firm.

Brush rolls all over with a little more egg. Using a sharp knife, cut each roll into 10 pieces (step 4) and place on trays. Bake for 25 minutes or until golden. Cool slightly.

Pipe noses on bears using extra barbecue sauce. Serve teddy bear rolls with tomato sauce.

STEP 1 Place a large log along the edge of one pastry sheet, leaving a 2cm border.

STEP 2 Place one thinner log on pastry sheet next to the enclosed log.

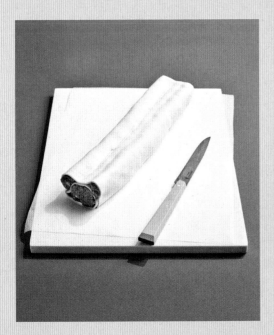

STEP 3 Using your hands, gently press along each ear line to form bear-shaped rolls.

STEP 4 Using a sharp knife, cut each roll into 10 pieces and place on trays.

RAINBOW DIP CUPS

2 x 400g cans chickpeas,
  drained, rinsed
1 small clove garlic
1 tsp vegetable stock powder
⅓ cup boiling water
¼ cup white sesame seeds
sliced red capsicum, baby cucumbers
  (qukes) and baby carrots, to serve

BEETROOT
1 cup chopped vacuum-packed
  cooked beetroot
⅓ cup finely grated parmesan
1 tbsp lemon juice

SPINACH
60g frozen spinach, thawed
2 tbsp chopped basil leaves
⅓ cup finely grated parmesan

CORN
1 cup sweet corn kernels, drained
⅓ cup finely grated parmesan
½ tsp turmeric (optional)

Process chickpeas, garlic, stock powder and the water until smooth. Divide chickpea mixture between three bowls. Proceed with flavour variations:

beetroot Process beetroot, parmesan, lemon juice and one portion of chickpea mixture until smooth; season. Return beetroot dip to bowl.

spinach Squeeze spinach until dry. Process spinach, basil, parmesan and one portion of chickpea mixture until smooth; season. Return spinach dip to bowl.

corn Process corn, parmesan, turmeric and remaining portion of chickpea mixture until smooth; season. Return corn dip to bowl.

Spoon beetroot dip evenly among eight ½-cup glasses or jars, then layer with spinach dip and corn dip. Sprinkle cups with sesame seeds.

Serve dip cups with vegie dippers. We used red capsicum, baby cucumbers and baby carrots.

PREP IT
Dips can be made a day ahead and stored separately, in airtight containers in the fridge.

FEEDS 16 WIGGLES

SSSSS-ANDWICHES

1 baguette
125g spreadable cream cheese,
  plus extra
9 tasty cheese slices, halved
200g shaved leg ham
5 small tomatoes, sliced thinly
20g baby spinach
¼ small red capsicum
1 black olive, sliced thinly
1 small cucumber, sliced thinly

Cut a 4cm piece from each end of the baguette; spread cut side of each piece with 1 teaspoon of the cream cheese. Make a horizontal cut in the rounded end of one piece, but do not cut all the way through; reserve both baguette pieces.

Slice remaining baguette into 2cm-thick slices. Spread each side of bread slices with remaining cream cheese.

Using the picture as a guide, position slices upright on a board in an S-shape to form a snake. Position the reserved piece of baguette with the cut at one end for the head and the other reserved piece at the other end for the tail.

Fill between each slice with cheese, ham, tomato and spinach.

Using the picture as a guide, trim a V-shape from capsicum piece for the tongue; position in the mouth as shown. Secure olive slices to cucumber rounds with a little extra cream cheese; position on the head for the eyes, securing with a little more cream cheese. Place a dot of extra cream cheese in the centre of the eyes for the pupils.

KEEP IT
Unfilled cookies will keep in an airtight container for up to 1 week.

MAKES 15 WIGGLY COOKIES

STRAWBERRIES & CREAM COOKIES

250g butter, softened
1 cup caster sugar
1 egg
3 tsp strawberry essence
2½ cups plain flour
pink food colouring
230g classic cream cheese icing
3 chocolate mint sticks, cut into
  2cm lengths (see Wiggly tip)
white writing gel

Beat butter and sugar in a medium bowl with an electric mixer until light and fluffy. Beat in egg and essence. Stir in sifted flour until a dough just forms. Turn dough out onto a lightly floured surface. Add a few drops of pink food colouring, then knead until dough is smooth and evenly coloured. Shape into a disc and wrap in plastic wrap. Refrigerate for 30 minutes.

Preheat oven to 180°C. Grease two large oven trays; line with baking paper.

Roll dough between two sheets of baking paper until 5mm thick. Using a 6cm round cutter, cut out 30 rounds from dough; place on trays 6cm apart. Using fingertips, pinch the base of each round to form a strawberry shape. Freeze for 30 minutes.

Bake cookies for 12 minutes or until they can be gently pushed without breaking. Leave on trays for 5 minutes before transferring to a wire rack to cool completely.

Spoon 1 teaspoon of the cream cheese icing onto the flat side of half the cooled cookies, then top with remaining cookies, flat-side down. Push a mint stick into icing at the top of each cookie for the stem. Using the writing gel, pipe tiny dots onto the cookies to resemble strawberry seeds; allow to set.

Wiggly tip Swap out mint sticks for chocolate pocky sticks, if you like. Pocky sticks are available at major supermarkets.

TEAPOT CAKE

STEP 1 Sandwich wider ends of cakes together with ½ cup of the icing to create a teapot shape.

STEP 2 With lightly oiled hands, shape rice puffs mixture into a teapot spout and handle.

STEP 3 Roll up a 15cm piece of licorice for the teapot knob to place on top of the teapot.

STEP 4 Cut 1.5cm rounds from sour strap to decorate the teapot.

PREP + COOK TIME
OVER
1 HR
+ COOLING

FEEDS 12 WIGGLES

TEAPOT CAKE

2 x 440g packets butter cake mix
100g marshmallows
45g rice puffs
7 bamboo skewers
black licorice strap
4 red sour straps

ICING
250g butter, softened
3 cups pure icing sugar, sifted
2 tbsp hot water
yellow and pink food colouring

Preheat oven to 180°C. Grease two 3-cup pudding steamers (7cm base, 16cm top, 6.5cm deep); dust with a little flour and shake out excess.

Prepare cake mixes according to packet directions. Divide mixture evenly between steamers (see Wiggly tips). Bake for 45 minutes or until a skewer inserted into the centre comes out clean. Leave in steamers for 10 minutes before turning out onto a wire rack to cool completely.

Meanwhile, to make icing, beat butter in a small bowl with an electric mixer until as pale as possible. Gradually beat in half the icing sugar, the water, then remaining icing sugar. Reserve ¾ cup of icing. Divide remaining icing between two bowls; tint one bowl yellow and the other bowl pink. Mix each bowl well to combine. Cover and stand at room temperature until needed.

Using a serrated knife, level cake tops if necessary. Sandwich wider ends of cakes together with ½ cup of the reserved icing to create a teapot shape, as shown in step 1 (page 31); secure to a cake board with a little more of the reserved icing. Spread pink icing all over cake to cover completely.

Wiggly tips To ensure the cakes are exactly the same size, use kitchen scales to weigh the cake mixture equally into the pudding steamers. We used a 1.5cm metal plain piping nozzle to cut the rounds from the sour straps to decorate the teapot.

Place marshmallows in a microwave-safe heatproof bowl; microwave on HIGH (100%) in 20-second bursts, stirring, until melted. Add rice puffs and fold through. Set aside for 10 minutes. With lightly oiled hands, shape rice puffs mixture into a teapot spout and handle, as shown in step 2 (page 31). Insert 3 skewers three-quarters of the way into the flat end of the spout and 2 skewers three-quarters of the way into each end of the handle. Insert spout and handle into cake, as shown on page 30; allow to set. Spread yellow icing all over spout and handle to cover.

Trim and shape a 35cm length of licorice to fit around the top of the teapot for the lid, as shown on page 30. Roll up a 15cm piece of licorice and place on top of the teapot for the teapot knob, as shown in step 3 (page 31). Cut 1.5cm rounds from sour straps (see Wiggly tips) to decorate the teapot, as shown in step 4 (page 31).

candy hearts

CUTIE PIE

foil horn

GOODY BAGS

These pretty party bags filled with sweet little treats and activities will have your guests enjoying the high tea life at home.

Make **Teddy Bear Cookies** with 1 quantity Take-home Wiggly Cookies (recipe page 54) and a 9.5cm x 7cm teddy bear head cutter. Make the icing, tinting it with brown food colouring instead. Ice the cookies as pictured and scatter with toasted desiccated coconut. Use mini jelly beans for the eyes and nose.

hot chocolate kit
(includes milk
powder, drinking
chocolate
and mini
marshmallows)

glitter

paint set

macarons

paper party bag

LOLLIES

Teddy Bear Cookies

LITTLE CHEFS

It's [name] birthday! We've cooked up some fun and yummy food. So join us to help them celebrate turning [age].

WHEN

You're ready for a culinary adventure!

TIME

Munch time

WHERE

Chez Wiggly House

DRESS UP

Chef's jacket and chef's hat

PLEASE BRING

Your appetite

MAKES 12 WIGGLY TACOS

BEEF TACOS

2 tsp olive oil
500g beef mince
1 clove garlic, crushed
2 tbsp tomato paste
2 tsp paprika
1 tsp ground cumin
12 corn taco shells
1 cup coarsely grated cheddar
8 cos lettuce leaves, shredded
2 medium tomatoes, chopped finely
mashed avocado and lime halves,
  to serve

Preheat oven to 180°C.

Heat oil in a large frying pan over medium heat. Add beef and garlic; cook, stirring with a wooden spoon to break up lumps, for 5 minutes or until beef is browned. Add 1½ cups water, tomato paste, paprika and cumin; stir until well combined. Season. Bring to the boil; reduce heat and simmer for 10 minutes or until most of the liquid is evaporated.

Meanwhile, place taco shells on a large oven tray and place in oven for 5 minutes or until shells are warmed.

Divide mince mixture among taco shells, then top with cheddar, lettuce and tomato. Serve tacos with mashed avocado and lime halves.

GOURMET TOMATO PIZZAS

7g sachet dry yeast
1 tsp caster sugar
1 cup (250ml) warm water
1 cup wholemeal plain flour
1¼ cups plain flour
1 tsp sea salt
1 tbsp olive oil, plus extra to drizzle
cooking oil spray
⅔ cup pizza sauce
320g mixed baby cherry tomatoes, halved
⅓ cup sliced kalamata olives
220g cherry bocconcini, drained
40g baby rocket leaves

Place yeast, sugar and the water in a small jug; stir to combine. Cover with plastic wrap and stand in a warm place for 10 minutes or until frothy.

Combine flours, salt, olive oil and yeast mixture in the bowl of an electric mixer fitted with a dough hook. Mix on low speed until just combined. Increase speed to medium; mix for 7 minutes or until dough is smooth and elastic. Transfer to an oiled large bowl; cover with plastic wrap or a clean tea towel and stand in a warm place for 45 minutes or until doubled in size.

Preheat oven to 220°C. Lightly spray two large oven trays with cooking oil spray.

Turn dough out onto a lightly floured surface; knead for 30 seconds or until smooth. Divide into four portions; roll each portion into a 15cm round. Place two dough rounds on each tray.

Using the back of a spoon, spread 2 tablespoons of the pizza sauce over base of each dough round until almost to the edge. Top with cherry tomatoes, olives and bocconcini; season. Bake for 18 minutes or until bocconcini is melted and bases are browned and crisp.

Serve pizzas topped with rocket and drizzled with extra olive oil.

MAKES 20 WIGGLY KNOTS

GARLIC BREAD KNOTS

250g store-bought fresh pizza dough
40g butter
1 clove garlic, crushed
1 tbsp chopped flat-leaf parsley
2 tbsp grated parmesan

Preheat oven to 200°C. Line two large oven trays with baking paper.

On a lightly floured surface, roll each piece of dough into a 12cm x 30cm rectangle. With a long side facing you, cut dough in half lengthways; cut each half crossways into 3cm-wide strips to make 20 strips in total.

Roll each strip into a 16cm-long rope, then twist each rope into a knot (not too tight); place on baking trays.

Place butter in a microwave-safe bowl; microwave on MEDIUM (80%) in 20-second bursts, stirring, until melted. Stir in garlic and parsley until combined.

Brush three-quarters of the garlic butter over top of knots, then sprinkle with parmesan. Bake for 15 minutes or until golden brown and cooked through. Brush with remaining garlic butter.

PREP + COOK TIME
UNDER 30 MINS

MAKES 16 WIGGLY POPPERS

HAMBURGER POPPERS

1 egg, beaten lightly
1 medium onion, grated
500g beef mince
½ cup stale breadcrumbs
2 tbsp worcestershire sauce
2 tbsp finely chopped parsley
2 tsp olive oil
4 tasty cheese slices
8 oak lettuce leaves
4 cocktail truss tomatoes
16 bread and butter pickle slices
16 bamboo cocktail skewers
tomato sauce, to serve

Place egg, onion, beef, breadcrumbs, worcestershire sauce and parsley in a large bowl, then season; mix until well combined. Divide beef mixture into 16 equal portions, then roll into balls; place on a tray lined with baking paper. Press down gently on balls to flatten slightly.

Heat oil in a large frying pan over medium heat; cook patties for 5 minutes, turning, until browned all over and cooked through. Cut each slice of cheese into four squares. Place a square of cheese on top of each patty; cook until cheese just melts.

Cut each lettuce leaf in half, then fold each piece into a little square. Cut each tomato into four slices. Top each patty with a lettuce square, a slice of tomato and a pickle slice; insert a cocktail skewer through each hamburger popper to hold everything together.

Serve hamburger poppers with tomato sauce.

BUTTERMILK WAFFLES

75g butter

1½ cups buttermilk

2 eggs

1 tsp vanilla extract

1½ cups wholemeal plain flour

¼ cup caster sugar

2 tsp baking powder

¼ tsp salt

cooking oil spray

halved bananas, blueberries,
  vanilla yoghurt and maple syrup,
  to serve

Place butter in a microwave-safe bowl; microwave on MEDIUM (80%) in 20-second bursts, stirring, until melted. Cool.

Preheat a 2-slice waffle maker.

Whisk melted butter, buttermilk, eggs and vanilla in a medium jug until well combined. Combine sifted flour, sugar, baking powder and salt in a medium bowl. Make a well in the centre of the flour mixture. Slowly pour buttermilk mixture into the well, whisking until batter is combined, thick and lumpy.

Lightly spray top and bottom of waffle maker with cooking oil spray. Pour ½ cup of batter into the centre of each waffle mould. Close the lid; cook for 3 minutes or until golden brown. Transfer waffles to a plate and cover to keep warm. Repeat cooking with remaining batter, spraying waffle maker between batches with more cooking oil spray, to make 6 waffles in total.

Serve waffles topped with halved bananas, blueberries and yoghurt, drizzled with maple syrup.

SMOOTHIES

PRETTY IN PINK

MAKES 2 WIGGLY SMOOTHIES

Peel and chop 1 large banana and place in a zip-lock plastic bag; freeze for 3 hours or until firm. Blend frozen banana, 2 cups frozen strawberries, 1 cup milk, ½ cup thick Greek yoghurt and 2 teaspoons honey in a blender on high speed until smooth. Divide smoothie between two glasses to serve.

PURPLE POWER

MAKES 2 WIGGLY SMOOTHIES

Peel and chop 1 small banana and place in a zip-lock plastic bag with ⅓ cup red grapes; freeze for 3 hours or until firm. Blend frozen banana and grapes, ⅓ cup frozen blueberries, ⅓ cup frozen blackberries, ½ cup milk, ½ cup thick Greek yoghurt and 8 ice cubes in a blender on high speed until smooth. Divide smoothie between two glasses to serve.

CALYPSO

MAKES 2 WIGGLY SMOOTHIES

Peel, core and chop half a small pineapple into small pieces. Blend pineapple, 1 cup frozen raspberries, ½ cup frozen mango pieces and 1 cup chilled coconut milk in a blender on high speed until smooth. Divide smoothie between two glasses to serve.

Wiggly tip For Calypso and Ruby Red smoothies, using a combination of coconut and rice milks will make them easier to blend.

RUBY RED

MAKES 2 WIGGLY SMOOTHIES

Peel and chop 1 medium banana and place in a zip-lock plastic bag; freeze for 3 hours or until firm. Wash, peel and chop 1 medium beetroot. Blend frozen banana, beetroot, 1 cup frozen blueberries, ½ cup baby spinach and 1 cup chilled coconut milk in a blender on high speed until smooth. Divide smoothie between two glasses to serve.

WIGGLY TIP
We used sugar-coated chocolate buttons and gobstoppers to decorate the top of the cake.

FEEDS 16 WIGGLES

WIGGLY RAINBOW CAKE

4 x 470g packets vanilla cake mix
purple, yellow, blue and red
  gel food colouring
assorted lollies (see Wiggly tip)
  and candles, to decorate
BUTTERCREAM
250g butter, softened
3 cups pure icing sugar, sifted
¼ cup milk

Preheat oven to 160°C. Grease two 20cm round cake pans; line bases and sides with baking paper.

Prepare cakes mixes according to packet directions, placing each cake batter in a separate bowl; tint one bowl purple, one yellow, one blue and one red. Mix each bowl well to combine.

Working with two coloured cake batters at a time, spread into pans. Bake for 40 minutes or until a skewer inserted into the centre comes out clean. Leave in pans for 5 minutes before turning out onto wire racks to cool completely. Wash, dry, grease and reline cake pans with baking paper. Repeat baking remaining two cake batters.

Meanwhile, to make buttercream, beat butter in a small bowl with an electric mixer until as pale as possible. Gradually beat in half the icing sugar, the milk, then remaining icing sugar. Cover and stand at room temperature until needed.

Using a serrated knife, level cake tops so cakes are the same height. Working with one cake at a time, place an 18cm round plate or cake pan on top of cake and carefully trim the side to expose the vibrant colour. Repeat trimming with remaining cakes.

Secure purple cake to a cake board with a little buttercream. Pipe or spread top with ¾ cup of buttercream. Continue layering with remaining cakes and buttercream. Decorate top of cake with remaining buttercream, assorted lollies and candles.

Prep it Cakes and buttercream can be made a day ahead and assembled on the day of the party. Store cakes in an airtight container at room temperature and refrigerate the buttercream. Allow buttercream to come to room temperature before using.

GOODY BAGS

Take-home Wiggly Cookies

MAKES 16 WIGGLY COOKIES

PREP + COOK TIME
UNDER 45 MINS
+ REFRIGERATION & COOLING

TAKE-HOME WIGGLY COOKIES

250g cold butter, chopped
1 cup pure icing sugar, sifted
2½ cups plain flour, sifted

ICING

2½ cups pure icing sugar
1 tbsp lemon juice, approximately
red, blue, yellow and purple
  gel food colouring

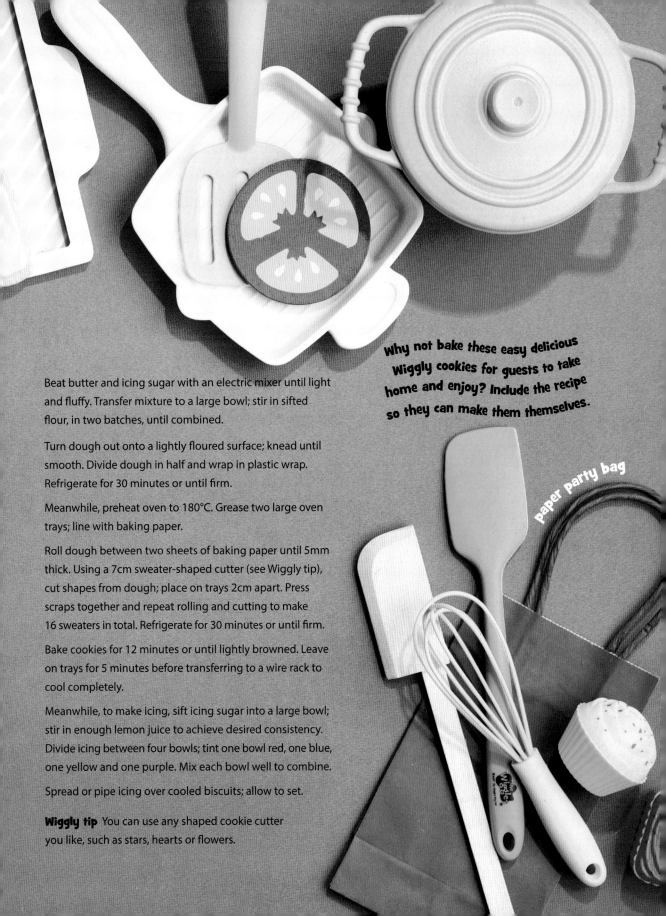

Why not bake these easy delicious Wiggly cookies for guests to take home and enjoy? Include the recipe so they can make them themselves.

paper party bag

Beat butter and icing sugar with an electric mixer until light and fluffy. Transfer mixture to a large bowl; stir in sifted flour, in two batches, until combined.

Turn dough out onto a lightly floured surface; knead until smooth. Divide dough in half and wrap in plastic wrap. Refrigerate for 30 minutes or until firm.

Meanwhile, preheat oven to 180°C. Grease two large oven trays; line with baking paper.

Roll dough between two sheets of baking paper until 5mm thick. Using a 7cm sweater-shaped cutter (see Wiggly tip), cut shapes from dough; place on trays 2cm apart. Press scraps together and repeat rolling and cutting to make 16 sweaters in total. Refrigerate for 30 minutes or until firm.

Bake cookies for 12 minutes or until lightly browned. Leave on trays for 5 minutes before transferring to a wire rack to cool completely.

Meanwhile, to make icing, sift icing sugar into a large bowl; stir in enough lemon juice to achieve desired consistency. Divide icing between four bowls; tint one bowl red, one blue, one yellow and one purple. Mix each bowl well to combine.

Spread or pipe icing over cooled biscuits; allow to set.

Wiggly tip You can use any shaped cookie cutter you like, such as stars, hearts or flowers.

PYJAMA PARTY

It's a sleepover birthday party! So get all snuggly in your pyjamas and join us to celebrate [name] turning [age]

WHEN

You're ready to stay awake and have fun ALL night

WHERE

Pillow fort in the living room

PLEASE BRING

Your favourite teddy and toothbrush

TIME

Night-time

DRESS UP

Pyjamas

PREP + COOK TIME
UNDER
15 MINS
+ FREEZING

MAKES 12 WIGGLY SPLITS

BANANA SPLIT ON A STICK

6 medium bananas
12 popsicle sticks
½ cup thickened cream
½ cup 100's & 1000's
200g milk chocolate, chopped
1 tbsp coconut oil
12 maraschino cherries with stalks

Line a large tray with baking paper. Peel bananas and cut in half crossways. Lay bananas on tray in a single layer; carefully push a popsicle stick into the curved end of each banana. Freeze for 1 hour.

Meanwhile, beat cream in a small bowl with an electric mixer until firm peaks form; spoon mixture into a piping bag fitted with a star nozzle. Refrigerate until needed.

Pour 100's & 1000's into a small bowl.

Place chocolate and coconut oil in a small microwave-safe jug; microwave on MEDIUM (80%) in 30-second bursts, stirring, until chocolate is melted. Cool slightly.

Working quickly, dip top end of bananas three-quarters into chocolate, then roll in 100's & 1000's; return to tray. Freeze for a further 15 minutes or until chocolate sets.

When ready to serve, pipe whipped cream on top of 100's & 1000's and press a cherry into the top of the cream.

Wiggly tip If chocolate starts to set, reheat in microwave in 10-second bursts, stirring, until melted.

FEEDS 8 WIGGLES

POP POP POPCORN

2 tbsp olive oil
1 cup popping corn
1 tsp sea salt flakes

CINNAMON DOUGHNUT
2 tbsp icing sugar mixture
¼ tsp sea salt flakes
½ tsp ground cinnamon
cooking oil spray

CHEESY CORN
80g cheese puffs
cooking oil spray

TEX-MEX
30g taco spice mix
2 tsp sea salt flakes
½ cup finely grated parmesan
cooking oil spray

Heat oil in a large heavy-based saucepan over medium heat; add popping corn and salt. Cover with a tight-fitting lid; cook, shaking pan occasionally, for about 4 minutes or until popping sound has stopped. Divide popcorn among three large bowls. Proceed with flavour variations:

cinnamon doughnut Sift icing sugar into a small bowl, then add salt and cinnamon; stir to combine. Spray popcorn generously with cooking oil spray. Sprinkle cinnamon mixture over popcorn; toss to coat well.

cheesy corn Place cheese puffs in a large zip-lock plastic bag; using a rolling pin, crush the puffs into fine crumbs. Spray popcorn generously with cooking oil spray. Sprinkle crushed cheese puff crumbs over popcorn; toss to coat well.

tex-mex Place spice mix, salt and parmesan in a small bowl; stir to combine. Spray popcorn generously with cooking oil spray. Sprinkle taco spice mixture over popcorn; toss to coat well.

PREP + COOK TIME
UNDER 30 MINS

MAKES 16 WIGGLY BAOS

BIRTHDAY BAOS

200g chicken tenderloins
¼ cup plain flour
1 egg
1 cup panko breadcrumbs
cooking oil spray
16 x 6cm mini bao buns
   (see Wiggly tip)
¼ cup hoisin sauce
1 medium carrot, julienned
4 baby cucumbers (qukes),
   cut into batons
japanese mayonnaise, to serve

Preheat oven to 200°C. Line a large oven tray with baking paper.

Cut chicken into sixteen 2cm x 5cm strips.

Place flour in a shallow bowl; season. Lightly beat egg in a second shallow bowl and place breadcrumbs in a third shallow bowl. Lightly dust chicken in flour; shake off excess. Working with one strip at a time, dip floured chicken in egg, then coat in breadcrumbs; place on tray in a single layer. Spray crumbed chicken with cooking oil spray. Bake for 12 minutes or until golden and cooked through.

Meanwhile, steam or microwave bao buns according to packet directions. Spread base of each bao bun with 1 teaspoon of the hoisin sauce, then top with a chicken strip, carrot and cucumber. Serve drizzled with mayonnaise.

Wiggly tip Bao buns are available from Asian grocers and major supermarkets.

MAKES 20 WIGGLY WONTONS

MEATBALL WONTON FLOWERS

250g pork mince
2 tbsp fine breadcrumbs
1 clove garlic, crushed
2 tsp finely grated ginger
2 tsp soy sauce
1 green onion, sliced thinly
1 egg yolk
40 x 8cm square egg wonton
   wrappers (see Wiggly tips)
cooking oil spray
1 punnet baby cucumbers (qukes)
10 cherry tomatoes, halved
sweet chilli sauce, to serve

Preheat oven to 180°C. Line two large oven trays with baking paper.

Place pork, breadcrumbs, garlic, ginger, soy sauce, green onion and egg yolk in a medium bowl, then season; mix to combine. Place 20 wonton wrappers on a clean surface; brush the centre of each with a little water, then top with a second wrapper on the diagonal to form a star shape. Spoon a level teaspoon of pork mixture in the centre of each wrapper; brush around mixture with a little water. Bring wrapper edges up to enclose filling; pinch to seal.

Carefully flatten wontons; place on trays, flat-side down. Spray with cooking oil spray. Bake for 12 minutes or until golden and crisp. Transfer to a wire rack to cool.

Meanwhile, to make flower stems, using a sharp knife, slice cucumbers in half lengthways, then cut three strips three-quarters of the way down each cucumber half, being careful not to cut all the way through. Gently separate strips.

Arrange wontons, flat-side up, at the end of cucumber stems for the flowers, then place a tomato half in the centre of each wonton. Serve with sweet chilli sauce.

Wiggly tips Square egg wonton wrappers are available from Asian grocers and major supermarkets. For the hungry caterpillar, arrange four baby orange grape tomatoes in a caterpillar shape, then top with an edible candy eyeball, securing with a little sweet chilli sauce.

WIGGLY TIPS
You will need ¼ cup blueberry puree. Toss doughnut centres in cinnamon sugar while warm and enjoy! Doughnuts are best eaten on day of making.

AIR FRYER DOUGHNUTS

10g dry yeast
¼ cup lukewarm water
80g butter, chopped
1 cup milk
¼ cup caster sugar
½ tsp salt
2 egg yolks
3 cups plain flour, sifted
cooking oil spray
sprinkles, to decorate

ICING
1 cup frozen blueberries, thawed
  (see Wiggly tips)
1¾ cups pure icing sugar, sifted

Combine yeast and the water in a small bowl; stir until yeast dissolves.

Place butter and milk in a microwave-safe jug; microwave on MEDIUM (80%) in 30-second bursts, stirring, until butter is melted. Cool until lukewarm.

Place yeast mixture, butter mixture, sugar, salt, egg yolks and flour in a large bowl; beat with a wooden spoon until mixture forms a soft, sticky dough. Cover and stand in a warm place for 1 hour or until doubled in size.

Turn dough out onto a lightly floured surface; knead gently until smooth, then roll out until approximately 1.5cm thick. Cut rounds from dough with a floured 7cm round cutter, then remove the centres with a floured 3.5cm round cutter. Press scraps together and repeat rolling and cutting to make 12 doughnuts in total. Place doughnuts and doughnut centres on oven trays lined with baking paper. Stand for 30 minutes or until risen slightly.

Meanwhile, to make icing, place blueberries in a medium bowl; using a fork, mash into a puree, then strain into a medium bowl. Discard pulp and skins. Add icing sugar to bowl; whisk until smooth. Cover and stand at room temperature until needed.

Preheat a 7-litre air fryer to 180°C for 3 minutes. Spray air fryer basket with cooking oil spray. Working in batches, cook doughnuts for 7 minutes and doughnut centres for 3 minutes, or until golden and a skewer inserted into the doughnut comes out clean. Cool completely.

Dip doughnut tops in icing one at a time; place on a wire rack. Scatter with sprinkles; allow to set.

MAKES ABOUT 15 WIGGLY WINGS

CHICKEN DRUMETTES

2 tbsp butter chicken curry paste
¾ cup Greek yoghurt
1kg chicken wing nibbles
lime wedges, to serve

RAITA
1 Lebanese cucumber
1 tbsp mint leaves
¾ cup Greek yoghurt
1 tbsp lemon juice

Preheat oven to 200°C. Line a large oven tray with baking paper.

Combine curry paste and yoghurt in a large bowl; season. Add chicken; mix to coat well. Place chicken on tray in a single layer. Bake for 30 minutes or until golden brown and cooked through.

Meanwhile, to make raita, coarsely grate cucumber and place in a colander. Using clean hands, squeeze out as much liquid as possible. Coarsely chop mint. Place yoghurt and lemon juice in a bowl, then season; stir to combine. Top yoghurt mixture with cucumber and mint. Cover and refrigerate until needed. When ready to serve, stir cucumber and mint into the yoghurt.

Serve chicken with raita and lime wedges.

KEYBOARD
CAKE

STEP 1 Tint one bowl of icing red, one yellow, one blue and one purple.

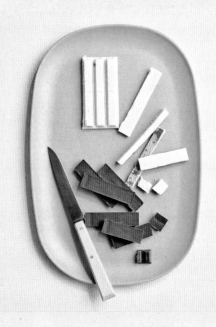

STEP 2 Cut each wafer bar finger into 7cm lengths. Cut each milk chocolate bar into 4.5cm lengths.

STEP 3 Place the smaller cake on top of the larger cake to form a keyboard shape.

STEP 4 Mark four 7cm wide sections on cake and spread each with a different coloured icing.

FEEDS 20 WIGGLES

KEYBOARD CAKE

3 x 440g packets butter cake mix
2 x 170g blocks white chocolate-coated
  wafer bars (see Wiggly tip)
200g white chocolate melts
1 tbsp canola oil
8 x 12.5g milk chocolate bars filled with
  a creamy milk centre (see Wiggly tip)
black licorice strap
12 mini brown sugar-coated chocolate buttons
9 brown sugar-coated chocolate buttons
ICING
250g unsalted butter, softened
3 cups pure icing sugar, sifted
2 tbsp hot water
red, yellow, blue and purple
  gel food colouring

Preheat oven to 180°C. Grease a 26cm x 35cm rectangular baking dish; line base and sides with baking paper.

Prepare cake mixes according to packet directions. Spread mixture into pan. Bake for 1 hour or until a skewer inserted into the centre comes out clean. Leave in pan for 5 minutes before turning out onto a wire rack to cool.

Meanwhile, to make icing, beat butter in a small bowl with an electric mixer until as pale as possible. Gradually beat in half the icing sugar, the water, then remaining icing sugar. Reserve ¼ cup of icing. Divide remaining icing between four bowls; tint one bowl red, one yellow, one blue and one purple, as shown in step 1 (page 73). Cover and stand at room temperature until needed.

Separate 14 fingers from wafer bar blocks; using a sharp knife, cut each finger into 7cm lengths, as shown in step 2 (page 73). Cut each milk chocolate bar into 4.5cm lengths.

Wiggly tip White chocolate-coated wafer bars and creamy milk-centred milk chocolate bars can be found at supermarkets and online.

Using a serrated knife, level cake top. Trim cake into a 20cm x 28cm rectangle, then cut a 5cm x 28cm rectangle from one of the long sides. Secure the larger cake, cut-side down, to a cake board with a little of the reserved icing, then place the smaller cake on top, cut-side down, to form a keyboard shape, as shown in step 3 (page 73). Mark four 7cm wide sections on the cake and spread each with a different coloured icing, over the top and sides, as shown in step 4 (page 73).

Press wafer bar fingers, flat-side up, into the bottom portion of the cake, as shown on page 72, then top with chocolate bar pieces, flat-side up, for the keys; secure with a little of the reserved icing.

Cut licorice into two 4cm rectangles; position on cake for the on/off buttons. Decorate keyboard with mini brown and brown chocolate buttons, as shown on page 72.

HOT CHOCOLATE

CREAMY MILK CHOCOLATE

MAKES 6 HOT CHOCOLATES

Coarsely chop 100g milk chocolate. Place 3 cups milk and 1 cup pouring cream in a medium heavy-based saucepan over medium heat. When mixture just begins to bubble around the edges, reduce heat to low. Whisk in 2 tablespoons sifted cocoa powder and the chopped chocolate. Cook for 3 minutes, stirring, until chocolate mixture is smooth and creamy. Remove from heat. Serve hot chocolate in mugs.

S'MORES

MAKES 6 HOT CHOCOLATES

Make Creamy Milk Chocolate recipe to left, adding ½ cup chocolate spread to hot chocolate mixture once pan is removed from heat; whisk until smooth and thick. Serve hot chocolate in mugs; top each with 2 white marshmallows.

CARAMEL WAFER

MAKES 6 HOT CHOCOLATES

Make Creamy Milk Chocolate recipe to left, whisking in ½ cup store-bought dulce de leche at the end until melted and combined. Whip 125ml thickened cream with an electric mixer until soft peaks form (cream just holds its shape when dropped from a spoon). Serve hot chocolate in mugs; top each with a spoonful of whipped cream and sprinkle with a crushed wafer roll biscuit. Serve each with 2 wafer roll biscuits for dipping and sipping.

STRAWBERRIES & CREAM

MAKES 6 HOT CHOCOLATES

Coarsely chop 80g white chocolate. Place 2 cups each strawberry milk and pouring cream in a medium heavy-based saucepan over medium heat. When mixture just begins to bubble around the edges, reduce heat to low. Whisk in chopped chocolate and 1 teaspoon vanilla extract. Cook for 3 minutes, stirring, until smooth and creamy. Remove from heat. Whip 125ml thickened cream with an electric mixer until soft peaks form. Serve hot chocolate in mugs; top each with a spoonful of whipped cream, crushed freeze-dried strawberries and sliced fresh strawberries.

popcorn

jelly beans

Just because the sleepover is over doesn't mean the party has to end! Pack your goody bags with lots of cool stuff to keep the fun going.

To make **Homemade Playdough** combine 1 cup plain flour, 2 teaspoons cream of tartar and ½ cup salt in a large bowl; set aside. Mix a few drops of food colouring and 1 cup water in a large saucepan, then stir in 1 tablespoon vegetable oil. Add dry ingredients to pan; mix well to combine. Cook over low-medium heat until a dough begins to form. When dough starts to come away from the side of the pan and form a ball, take off heat. Leave dough in pan to cool. Once cooled, knead for 5 minutes until softened. To keep soft, store playdough in an airtight container or zip-lock plastic bag.

whistles

colouring pencils

jointed snake toy

GOODY BAGS

Homemade Playdough

lollies on a stick

rainbow twist lollipop

paper party bag

party blowout

tennis ball

torch

UNDER THE SEA

It's [name] birthday and we're making a big splash about it! Join us for waves of fun at their [age] birthday party.

WHEN

You want to dive into a deep-sea adventure

TIME

At high tide

WHERE

X marks the spot

PLEASE BRING

Swimming goggles and a beach towel

DRESS UP

Swimsuit

MAKES 32 WIGGLY WRAPS

CURLY WURLY WRAPS

sweet chilli sauce, for dipping

CHICKEN & AVOCADO

1 small avocado, chopped

½ tsp lemon juice

2 regular wholegrain wraps

½ cup firmly packed shredded
   barbecued chicken

1 small carrot, grated

HAM & CHEESE

2 round spinach and herb wraps

⅓ cup spreadable cream cheese

100g shaved ham

1 small cucumber, cut into 8 batons

chicken and avocado Place avocado and lemon juice in a small bowl; mash with a fork until smooth. Season to taste. Lay wraps on a clean chopping board. Trim sides so they look like squares. Spread avocado mixture over wraps, leaving a 4cm border along the edge closest to you. Place chicken along the border, then top with carrot. Starting from the edge closest to you, roll up each wrap firmly, then wrap tightly in plastic wrap. Place rolls in the fridge for 10 minutes to firm up slightly.

ham and cheese wraps Lay wraps on a clean chopping board. Trim sides so they look like squares. Spread cream cheese over wraps, leaving a 4cm border along the edge closest to you. Place ham along the border, then top with cucumber. Starting from the edge closest to you, roll up each wrap firmly, then wrap tightly in plastic wrap. Place wraps in the fridge for 10 minutes to firm up slightly.

Remove plastic wrap from wraps. Using a sharp serrated knife, slice each wrap into 8 rounds. Serve with sweet chilli sauce.

MAKES 6 WIGGLY ROLLS

SAIL AWAY ROLLS

6 bake at home dinner rolls (300g)
3 slices swiss cheese
3 slices thick boneless ham
6 pretzel sticks
250g cream cheese, at room
  temperature
2 baby cucumbers (qukes),
  sliced thinly

Bake dinner rolls according to packet directions. Cool completely.

Meanwhile, cut large triangles from cheese and ham. Using a sharp knife, cut a slit in the top and bottom of each triangle. Thread a pretzel stick through slits for the sails (see Wiggly tip).

Using a sharp knife, cut out a wedge lengthways in the top of each roll; spread a heaped tablespoon of the cream cheese in each cavity. Position sails in the centre of the rolls, pressing pretzel sticks into rolls gently to secure. Arrange cucumber slices on cream cheese for the portholes.

Wiggly tip You may need two pretzel sticks to ensure the sails stand upright.

MAKES 16 WIGGLY ROCKS

SEA ROCKS

**2 cups desiccated coconut,
    plus 1 tbsp extra**
½ cup coconut cream
1 tbsp maple syrup
**2 x 225g packets dark or milk
    chocolate melts**
2 tsp vegetable oil

Place desiccated coconut, coconut cream and maple syrup in a medium bowl; mix until well combined. Using clean, damp hands, roll level tablespoons of mixture into 16 balls; place on a baking-paper-lined tray. Cover with plastic wrap and freeze until firm.

Place chocolate melts in a microwave-safe bowl; microwave on HIGH (100%) in 30-second bursts, stirring, until melted and smooth. Add oil; stir to combine. Cool slightly.

Using a fork, dip balls in chocolate, one at a time, until completely coated; drain off excess. Return to lined tray and sprinkle with extra desiccated coconut. Allow to set at room temperature.

WIGGLY TIP
Sea Rocks will keep in an airtight container in the fridge for up to 2 weeks.

WIGGLY TIP
You can use any firm white fish that you like for this recipe, such as ling, flathead or snapper.

MAKES 8 WIGGLY TACOS

FISH TACOS

200g packaged coleslaw
1 green onion, sliced thinly
⅓ cup whole-egg mayonnaise
8 small firm skinless boneless
  fish fillets (500g) (see Wiggly tip)
½ cup plain flour
2 tsp Mexican spice mix
2 eggs
1 cup mixed grain breadcrumbs
2 tbsp olive oil
8 regular white corn tortillas
sliced avocado, coriander leaves
  and lime halves, to serve

Place coleslaw, green onion and mayonnaise in a medium bowl; mix well to combine. Refrigerate until needed.

Cut fish into 2cm-wide strips. Combine flour and spice mix in a shallow bowl; season. Lightly beat eggs in a second shallow and place breadcrumbs in a third shallow bowl. Lightly dust fish in flour mixture; shake off excess. Working with one strip at a time, dip floured fish in egg, then coat in breadcrumbs.

Heat oil in a medium non-stick frying pan over medium heat. Working in batches, cook fish for 3 minutes each side or until golden and cooked through. Transfer to a plate lined with paper towel; cover to keep warm.

Warm tortillas in microwave according to packet directions. Divide fish strips among tortillas, then top with coleslaw, sliced avocado and coriander leaves. Serve with lime halves.

PREP + COOK TIME
UNDER 30 MINS

MAKES 6 WIGGLY CRÊPES

FISHY CRÊPES

1 cup milk
2 eggs
¾ cup plain flour
¼ tsp salt
40g butter
1½ tbsp lemon curd, plus extra
  (see Wiggly tips)
6 edible candy eyeballs
125g blueberries
mandarin segments, thinly sliced
  star fruit and raspberries,
  to decorate

Whisk milk and eggs in a large jug until well combined. Combine sifted flour and salt in a medium bowl. Make a well in the centre of the flour mixture. Slowly pour egg mixture into the well, whisking until batter is combined and smooth. Pour batter back into large jug.

Melt a little butter in a 20cm non-stick frying pan over medium-low heat. Pour ⅓ cup of batter into the pan, tilting to coat the base; cook over low heat for 1 minute or until browned lightly, loosening around the edge with a spatula. Turn crêpe; cook for 1 minute or until browned. Remove crêpe from pan; cover to keep warm. Repeat with remaining butter and batter to make 6 crêpes in total.

Spread crêpes with lemon curd, then fold in half to create a semi-circle. Fold semi-circle three times to create a triangle for the body. Place candy eyeballs on 6 blueberries, securing with a little extra lemon curd; position at pointy end of crêpes for the eyes. Decorate crêpes with remaining fruit.

Wiggly tips We spread our crêpes with lemon curd, but you can also try jam, hazelnut spread and smooth ricotta, if you like. If you are short on time, use pre-packaged crêpes.

MAKES 8 WIGGLY CROISSANTS

CRABWICHES

⅔ cup strawberry jam

8 mini croissants, halved horizontally

24 strawberries, halved lengthways
  (see Wiggly tip)

16 edible candy eyeballs

Spread 1 tablespoon of the jam over the base of each croissant; sandwich together with the lid.

Cut a V-shape from 16 strawberry halves for the claws. Slice remaining strawberry halves for the legs.

Arrange strawberry claws at the front of croissants and the legs at the back, as shown. Position candy eyeballs on croissant lids for the eyes, securing with a little extra jam.

WIGGLY TIP
You will need approximately 2½ punnets of strawberries.

PREP IT
Recipe can be made
to the end of step 5
a day ahead.

STARFISH JELLO CUPS

2 x 85g packets berry blue
   jelly crystals
10 strawberries, sliced thinly
¼ small papaya, sliced thinly
½ medium mango, sliced thinly
450g cream cheese, at room
   temperature
1 cup thick vanilla yoghurt
20g butter, melted
6 shortbread biscuits
⅓ cup desiccated coconut

Make jelly in a large jug according to packet directions.
Refrigerate for 1 hour or until jelly is partially set and the
consistency of unbeaten egg whites.

Meanwhile, using various sized star-shaped cutters
(see Wiggly tip), cut shapes from fruit.

Whisk cream cheese and yoghurt in a medium bowl
until smooth.

Divide yoghurt mixture evenly among 12 x 1-cup glasses;
arrange half the fruit stars flat on yoghurt mixture. Transfer
to a tray. Refrigerate for 30 minutes.

When jelly is partially set, carefully spoon over yoghurt mixture.
Refrigerate for 3 hours or until jelly sets completely.

Meanwhile, to make sand, place butter in a small microwave-
safe bowl; microwave on MEDIUM (80%) in 10-second bursts,
stirring, until melted. Cool slightly. Place biscuits in a zip-lock
plastic bag; using a rolling pin, crush biscuits into fine crumbs.
Add melted butter and coconut to bag; mix to combine.
Cool completely.

Just before serving, sprinkle sand over set jelly and top with
remaining fruit stars.

Wiggly tip We used 1cm and 2cm star-shaped cutters.

HENRY THE OCTOPUS CAKE

STEP 1 Using a serrated knife, trim top and side of cake to give a more rounded shape.

STEP 2 Place one end of legs inside cavity of cake, allowing other end to drape over the side.

STEP 3 Cut a round from each ice-cream wafer and stack together, securing with a little icing.

STEP 4 Arrange sour strap squares in a checkerboard pattern on legs.

FEEDS 16 WIGGLES

HENRY THE OCTOPUS CAKE

250g unsalted butter, softened

1¼ cups caster sugar

1 tsp vanilla extract

3 eggs

2½ cups self-raising flour

¾ cup milk

1 stroopwafel

5 ice-cream wafers

black licorice strap

160g packet red sour straps,
  cut into 1cm squares

160g packet blue sour straps,
  cut into 1cm squares

1 white marshmallow, halved horizontally

ICING

250g unsalted butter, softened

3 cups pure icing sugar, sifted

2 tbsp hot water

yellow and purple gel food colouring

Preheat oven to 180°C. Grease a 20cm round cake pan; line base and side with baking paper.

Beat butter, sugar and vanilla in the bowl of an electric mixer until pale and fluffy. Add eggs, one at a time, beating after each addition until just combined. Stir in sifted flour and milk, in two batches, until mixture is smooth. Spread mixture into pan. Bake for 1 hour or until a skewer inserted into the centre comes out clean. Leave in pan for 10 minutes before turning out onto a wire rack to cool completely.

Meanwhile, to make icing, beat butter in a small bowl with an electric mixer until as pale as possible. Gradually beat in half the sifted icing sugar, the water, then remaining icing sugar. Place half the icing in a medium bowl and tint yellow; reserve ¼ cup of icing. Place a quarter of the remaining icing in a second bowl and tint purple. Place the remaining icing in a third bowl and leave white. Cover and stand at room temperature until needed.

Using an 8.5cm round cutter, remove the centre from the cake; reserve. Using a serrated knife, trim top and side of cake to give a more rounded shape, as shown in step 1 (page 99); reserve offcuts. Secure cake to a cake board with a little of the reserved yellow icing; spread cake all over with yellow icing.

Place reserved cake centre and offcuts in a processer; pulse until fine crumbs form; reserve ¼ cup cake crumbs. Transfer remaining cake crumbs to a bowl

Prep it Cake and hat can be made the day before. Legs are best made close to decorating. Buttercream can be made the day before but it's best to tint close to decorating. You can cut the checkerboard shapes from the sour straps the day before too.

with ¾ cup of white icing; mix until well combined. Roll ¾ cup of mixture into a ball for the head. Roll remaining mixture into eight 12cm lengths for the legs.

Place one end of each leg inside the cavity of the cake, allowing the other end to drape over the side. Fill cavity with reserved cake crumbs, as shown in step 2 (page 99). Refrigerate cake and ball for 30 minutes.

Meanwhile, to make the hat, using a 5.5cm round cutter, cut out a round from the stroopwafel. Using a 3cm round cutter, cut a round from each ice-cream wafer; stack them together, securing with a little of the reserved yellow icing, as shown in step 3 (page 99). Place the stacked wafers in the centre of the stroopwafel round, securing with more reserved yellow icing. Cut licorice strap into the correct length to fit around the base of the hat; secure to hat with reserved yellow icing.

Carefully position head in the centre of the legs, securing with a little of the purple icing; spread purple icing all over the head.

Spread remaining white icing over the legs. Arrange red and blue sour strap squares in a checkerboard pattern on the legs, as shown in step 4 (page 99).

Using scissors, cut bow tie, mouth and shoes from licorice strap; position on cake, as shown on page 98. For the eyes, cut two rounds from licorice strap for the pupils, then top marshmallow halves with licorice rounds, securing with any leftover icing; position on face. Gently press hat onto Henry's head.

FRUITY LEMONADE

RED DELIGHT

MAKES 1 LITRE

Using a 3cm star-shaped cutter, cut shapes from 250g seedless watermelon. Place watermelon, 125g sliced strawberries, 60g raspberries, 3 cups chilled lemonade and 3 drops natural red food colouring (optional) in a large jug; stir to combine. Refrigerate until ready to serve. Serve fruity lemonade over crushed ice.

MELLOW YELLOW

MAKES 1 LITRE

Peel and core 1 small ripe pineapple. Using a 4cm flower-shaped cutter, cut shapes from pineapple. Thinly slice 2 star fruit and scoop out the pulp from 6 passionfruit. Place pineapple, star fruit, passionfruit pulp, 3 cups chilled lemonade and 3 drops natural yellow food colouring (optional) in a large jug; stir to combine. Refrigerate until ready to serve. Serve fruity lemonade over crushed ice.

GREEN MACHINE

MAKES 1 LITRE

Peel and slice 2 medium kiwifruit, thinly slice 1 small green apple and cut 150g seedless green grapes in half. Place kiwifruit, apple, grapes, 3 cups chilled lemonade and 3 drops natural green food colouring (optional) in a large jug; stir to combine. Refrigerate until ready to serve. Serve fruity lemonade over crushed ice.

BLUE LAGOON

MAKES 1 LITRE

Cut 150g seedless black grapes and 125g blackberries in half. Place 125g blueberries, the grapes, blackberries, 3 cups chilled lemonade and 3 drops natural blue food colouring (optional) in a large jug; stir to combine. Refrigerate until ready to serve. Serve fruity lemonade over crushed ice.

chocolate gold coins

pirate eye patch

GOODY BAGS

Another sea adventure awaits your guests with these goody bags overspilling with loot and all sorts of other yummy treasure.

To make **Edible Slime** combine 1 cup water, 1 tablespoon psyllium husk, 1 tablespoon icing sugar and a few drops of blue food colouring in a large microwave-safe bowl; stand at room temperature until husks absorb some of the water. Microwave on HIGH (100%) for 3 minutes, in 1-minute bursts, stirring, until mixture begins to bubble. Cool to room temperature, stirring occasionally. Store slime in sealable jars or an airtight container in the fridge for up to 1 week.

shell and starfish wands

party hat

paper party bag

Edible Slime

squeezy octopus toy

shell-shaped lollies

handball

ANIMAL
PARTY

It's time to go wild! All jungle buddies are invited to swing into [name] birthday party to help them celebrate turning [age]!

WHEN

You're ready to embark on a wild adventure

TIME

Grazing time

WHERE

At the jungle gym

PLEASE BRING

Your safari hat

DRESS UP

Animal onesie

MAKES 8 WIGGLY SUSHI

BEE SUSHI

1 cup sushi rice
½ tsp ground turmeric
1⅓ cups chicken stock
1 tbsp rice vinegar
2 tsp caster sugar
2 nori sheets
8 baked pretzel twists

Place rice in a sieve and rinse under cold running water until water runs clear. Place rice, turmeric and stock in a medium saucepan; bring to the boil. Reduce heat to low; cook, covered, for 20 minutes or until stock is absorbed. Remove from heat. Cover and stand for 5 minutes.

While rice is still hot, add combined vinegar and sugar; stir with a wooden spoon for 5 minutes or until sticky and cooled to room temperature. Using clean, damp hands, shape 2 tablespoons of rice mixture into oval shapes.

Cut 8 x 3mm thick strips lengthways from one nori sheet, then cut each strip in half crossways to make 16 strips in total. From the remaining nori sheet, using the tip of a 3mm plain piping tube, cut 16 circles for the eyes, then cut eight small thin strips for the mouth (see Wiggly tip).

Place two nori strips on each body to form stripes, then position eyes and mouth on bees. Trim pretzels to size for the antennae and press into the head, as shown.

WIGGLY TIP
Instead of using
scissors to cut out
nori shapes, nori
face stamps can be
purchased online or
in craft stores.

MAKES 14 WIGGLY PINWHEELS

PINWHEEL SNAILS

½ cup pizza sauce
1 tbsp sun-dried tomato pesto
2 x 250g store-bought
  fresh pizza dough
1 cup pizza cheese
cooking oil spray

Preheat oven to 180°C. Line two large oven trays with baking paper.

Combine pizza sauce and pesto in a small bowl; mix well.

Knead dough together on a lightly floured surface to form one ball; roll into a 30cm x 40cm rectangle.

With a long side facing you, spread pesto mixture evenly over dough, leaving a 2.5cm border on the opposite long side; scatter cheese over pesto mixture.

Roll up dough from the long side closest to you, up to the border to form a log with a flap; trim ends. Using a sharp knife, cut log into 2cm-thick slices; place, cut-side down, on trays. Slightly twist flaps on each slice. Using scissors, cut a V-shape from the end of each flap so they resemble antennae. Spray snails with oil. Bake for 18 minutes or until dough is browned and cooked through.

WIGGLY
CATERPILLAR
EMPANADAS

WIGGLY CATERPILLAR EMPANADAS

2 tsp olive oil
250g beef mince
½ cup frozen mixed vegetables, chopped
¾ cup tomato and basil pasta sauce
2 x 250g store-bought fresh pizza dough
1 egg, beaten lightly
1 black olive, chopped finely
kale leaves and tomato sauce, to serve

Heat oil in a medium frying pan over medium-high heat; add beef and cook, stirring with a wooden spoon to break up lumps, for 5 minutes or until browned. Add mixed vegetables and pasta sauce; bring to the boil. Reduce heat to low; cook, stirring, for 5 minutes or until thickened. Cool completely.

Preheat oven to 180°C. Line two large oven trays with baking paper.

Divide each dough ball into five equal portions (approximately 50g each). Working with one ball at a time, roll on a lightly floured surface into an 11cm x 15cm oval. With a long side facing you, spoon 1 tablespoon of filling along the long edge closest to you (step 1). Using a sharp knife, cut 5cm-thick strips halfway up the opposite long side (step 2). From the long side closest to you, roll dough over filling to enclose, then carefully roll up all the way to the end of the strips to form a log; place, cut-side up, on tray. Using your hands, gently bend log to create an S-shape for the caterpillar (step 3). Repeat with remaining dough and filling to make 10 caterpillars in total.

Brush tops of caterpillars with egg. Position olive pieces on caterpillars for the eyes. Bake for 18 minutes or until dough is browned and cooked through (step 4). Transfer to a wire rack to cool.

Arrange caterpillar empanadas on a bed of kale and serve with tomato sauce.

STEP 1 Spoon 1 tablespoon of filling along the long edge of dough.

STEP 2 Cut 5cm-thick strips halfway up the opposite long side of dough.

STEP 3 Using your hands, gently bend log to create an S-shape for the caterpillar.

STEP 4 Bake for 18 minutes or until dough is browned and cooked through.

PREP IT
Eggcellent Owls are best assembled just before serving.

PREP + COOK TIME UNDER 30 MINS

MAKES 4 WIGGLY RICE CAKES

EGGCELLENT OWLS

4 eggs
1 small apple
1 tsp lemon juice
4 thin rice cakes
⅓ cup mustard pickles
100g grated smoked cheddar
8 black sliced olives
8 each mini baked pretzel triangles
  and twists

Place eggs in a small saucepan and cover with cold water; bring to the boil over high heat. Boil for 12 minutes; drain. When cool enough to handle, peel eggs. Cool.

Halve, core and thinly slice apple; place in a small bowl and drizzle over lemon juice (this will stop the apple slices from turning brown).

Spread each rice cake with 1 tablespoon mustard pickles, then top with cheddar. Position an apple slice on each side of the rice cakes for the wings.

Carefully slice boiled eggs crossways. Using only the two middle slices from each egg, position on rice cakes for the eyes (reserve leftover egg for another use, see Wiggly tip). Place an olive slice on each egg slice for the pupils. Position 2 pretzel triangles on each owl for the beak and 2 twist pretzels for the feet.

Wiggly tip Roughly mash leftover eggs with yoghurt and mayonnaise to make creamy egg sandwiches.

BUGGY BITES

SNAILS

Cut 2 stalks celery into 6cm lengths; spread with ⅔ cup nut-free peanut butter spread. Cut 1 baby cucumber (quke) into slices. Position a cucumber slice upright on nut-free spread for the shell. Secure 2 candy eyeballs to each of 4 cherry tomatoes with nut-free spread; position on snails for the head. Cut 2 chives to the correct length and position on snails for the antennae.

BUTTERFLIES

Cut 1 stalk celery into 4cm lengths; spread with ⅓ cup spreadable cream cheese; top with ⅓ cup nut-free peanut butter. Cut 1 small cucumber into slices and trim a little; position on nut-free spread for the wings. Secure 2 candy eyeballs to each butterfly for the eyes. Cut 2 chives to the correct length and position on butterflies for the antennae.

DRAGONFLIES

Cut 2 stalks celery into 8cm lengths; spread with ½ cup nut-free peanut butter spread. Cut 2 baby carrots lengthways into thin slices and position on nut-free spread for the body. Cut 1 small cucumber into slices and trim a little; position on dragonflies for the wings. Secure 2 candy eyeballs to each dragonfly with a little nut-free spread for the eyes. Cut 2 chives to the correct length and position on dragonflies for the antennae.

LADY BUGS

Quarter 2 strawberries lengthways. Top 4 mini cheese rounds (encased in red wax) with 2 strawberry quarters each for the wings, securing with a little cream cheese. Secure 2 candy eyeballs to each of 4 small raspberries with a little more cream cheese for the eyes; position eyes on lady bugs, securing with cream cheese.

CATERPILLARS

Cut 2 stalks celery into 14cm lengths; spread with ⅔ cup nut-free peanut butter spread. Cut 6 baby cucumbers (qukes) into slices; position, overlapping, on nut-free spread for the body. Secure a candy eyeball to each caterpillar with a little nut-free spread for the eye. For a variation, use spreadable cream cheese instead of nut-free peanut butter spread and raspberries instead of cucumber slices. Secure 2 candy eyeballs to each caterpillar with cream cheese for the eyes.

SNAKES

Cut 2 stalks celery into 14cm lengths; spread with ½ cup spreadable cream cheese. Cut 12 strawberries into thin slices; position, overlapping, on cream cheese for the body. Secure 2 candy eyeballs to each snake with a little cream cheese for the eyes. For a variation, use baby cucumbers with a wedge cut out lengthways instead of celery and 1.5cm capsicum strips instead of strawberry slices. Trim capsicum pieces for the tongues.

WASPS

Halve 2 baby cucumbers (qukes) crossways; cut out a wedge lengthways from each half. Spread ⅔ cup spreadable cream cheese into cavities. Cut 1 small cucumber into slices and trim a little; position on wasps for the wings. Cut 4 cherry tomatoes in half; position two halves on each wasp for the body. Secure 2 candy eyeballs to each wasp with a little cream cheese for the eyes. Cut 2 chives to the correct length and position on wasps for the antennae.

snails

butterflies

dragonflies

lady bugs

caterpillars

snakes

wasps

caterpillars

snakes

PRED + COOK TIME

MAKES 10 WIGGLY HOT DOGS

GOOFY HOT DOGS

10 cocktail frankfurts
10 slices tasty cheese
5 slices devon
10 pitted black olives
10 brioche sliders (200g),
  halved horizontally
½ cup tomato sauce
20 edible candy eyeballs
5 tbsp American mustard
  (see Wiggly tip)
extra tomato sauce, to serve

Bring a small saucepan of water to the boil; add frankfurts. Cook for 5 minutes or until heated through; drain. Cover to keep warm.

Cut two 2.5cm x 8cm oval shapes from each slice of cheese and two 3cm x 5cm oval shapes from each slice of devon. Cut 5 olives in half lengthways and slice 10 x 5mm slices from remaining olives.

Secure cheese slices to slider tops with a little tomato sauce for the ears and olive halves to slider tops for the nose.

To make the eyes, secure candy eyeballs to olive slices with a little tomato sauce, then secure one eye on each slider top. Secure remaining candy eyeballs to slider tops with a little more tomato sauce.

Spread each slider base with 2 teaspoons mustard. Position devon slices on bases for the tongue, then place a frankfurt on each base; sandwich together with slider tops.

Serve hot dogs with extra tomato sauce.

WIGGLY TIP
Swap American mustard for barbecue sauce, if you like.

WAGS THE
DOG CAKE

WAGS THE DOG
CAKE TEMPLATE

Photocopy on A3 paper and
increase by 50%.

FEEDS 20 WIGGLES

WAGS THE DOG CAKE

3 x 440g packets chocolate cake mix
black licorice strap
1 white marshmallow, halved
BUTTERCREAM
250g unsalted butter, softened
3 cups pure icing sugar, sifted
2 tbsp hot water
red and brown gel food colouring

Preheat oven to 180°C. Grease a 26cm x 35cm rectangular baking dish; line base and sides with baking paper.

Prepare cake mixes according to packet directions. Spread mixture into pan. Bake for 1 hour or until a skewer inserted into the centre comes out clean. Leave in pan for 10 minutes before turning out onto a wire rack to cool.

Meanwhile, to make buttercream, beat butter in a small bowl with an electric mixer until as pale as possible. Gradually beat in half the icing sugar, the water, then remaining icing sugar. Place ⅓ cup of buttercream in a small bowl and tint pink. Place 1 cup of buttercream in a second bowl and tint light brown. Place remaining buttercream in a third bowl and tint dark brown. Cover and stand at room temperature until needed.

Level cake top, if necessary. Using a small, sharp knife, cut head and ears from cake using the template on page 125. Secure head, cut-side down, to a cake board with a little of the dark brown buttercream. Position ears on head, as shown on page 124, securing to cake board with more dark brown buttercream.

Wiggly tips Most packet cake mixes include a sachet of icing; you can use this instead of making the buttercream, if you like. Cake can be made the day before; store in an airtight container until ready to cut out. Make the Doggy Biscuits on page 130 to go with the cake.

Spread dark brown buttercream all over cake. Using the picture on page 124 as a guide, mark out the snout, mouth, tongue and inside ears with a skewer. Spread light brown buttercream on the snout and spots inside the ears. Spread inside the mouth with pink buttercream. Add more red colouring to remaining pink buttercream in bowl to tint dark red, then spread tongue with red buttercream.

Cut some licorice strap into the correct lengths to outline the face, ears, inside the ears, the snout and tongue; position on cake as shown on page 124. For the eyes, cut two ovals from more licorice strap; secure to marshmallow halves using a little more buttercream and position on cake. For the nose, cut two half circles from licorice strap and position on snout. Cut a length of licorice strap for the tongue groove and position on cake, as shown on page 124.

SLUSHIES

PINE LIME

MAKES 4 SLUSHIES

Blend 500g frozen pineapple pieces, ⅓ cup lime juice,
1 tablespoon honey and ¾ cup chilled sparkling water
in a blender until thick and smooth. Divide slushie
among four glasses to serve.

PINK LEMONADE

MAKES 4 SLUSHIES

Blend 500g frozen lemon sorbet, 1 cup frozen
strawberries, ⅓ cup lemon juice and ½ cup chilled
sparkling water in a blender until thick and smooth.
Divide slushie among four glasses to serve.

MANGO

MAKES 4 SLUSHIES

Blend 500g frozen mango chunks, 2 tablespoons
lime juice and ½ cup chilled sparkling water in
a blender until thick and smooth. Divide slushie
among four glasses to serve.

RASPBERRY

MAKES 4 SLUSHIES

Blend 500g frozen raspberries, ⅓ cup lemon juice,
2 tablespoons blackcurrant fruit juice syrup and ¾ cup
chilled sparkling water in a blender until thick and
smooth. Divide slushie among four glasses to serve.

lolly snakes

jointed snake toy

GOODY BAGS

It's a jungle out there, so don't send your guests away without supplies to keep them disguised, fed and entertained.

Make **Doggy Biscuits** with 1 quantity Take-home Wiggly Cookies (recipe page 54) and a 10cm bone-shaped cutter. Place icing in a piping bag with a fine nozzle. Pipe an outline 3mm in from cookie edge, then fill the inside with icing.

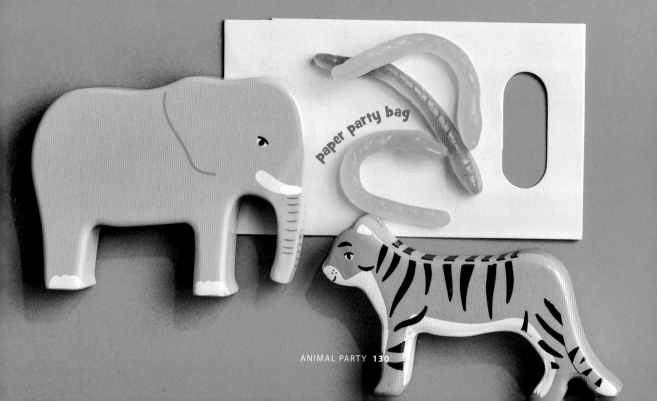

paper party bag

animal masks

Doggy Biscuits

craft kit

CONVERSION CHART

MEASURES

One Australian metric measuring cup holds approximately 250ml; one Australian metric tablespoon holds 20ml; one Australian metric teaspoon holds 5ml. The difference between one country's measuring cups and another's is within a two- or three-teaspoon variance and will not affect your cooking results. North America, New Zealand and the United Kingdom use a 15ml tablespoon.

All cup and spoon measurements are level. The most accurate way of measuring dry ingredients is to weigh them.

When measuring liquids, use a clear glass or plastic jug with the metric markings.

We use extra-large eggs with an average weight of 60g unless noted otherwise.

DRY MEASURES

metric	imperial
15g	½oz
30g	1oz
60g	2oz
90g	3oz
125g	4oz (¼lb)
155g	5oz
185g	6oz
220g	7oz
250g	8oz (½lb)
280g	9oz
315g	10oz
345g	11oz
375g	12oz (¾lb)
410g	13oz
440g	14oz
470g	15oz
500g	16oz (1lb)
750g	24oz (1½lb)
1kg	32oz (2lb)

LIQUID MEASURES

metric	imperial
30ml	1 fluid oz
60ml	2 fluid oz
100ml	3 fluid oz
125ml	4 fluid oz
150ml	5 fluid oz
190ml	6 fluid oz
250ml	8 fluid oz
300ml	10 fluid oz
500ml	16 fluid oz
600ml	20 fluid oz
1000ml (1 litre)	1¾ pints

LENGTH MEASURES

metric	imperial
3mm	⅛in
6mm	¼in
1cm	½in
2cm	¾in
2.5cm	1in
5cm	2in
6cm	2½in
8cm	3in
10cm	4in
13cm	5in
15cm	6in
18cm	7in
20cm	8in
22cm	9in
25cm	10in
28cm	11in
30cm	12in (1ft)

OVEN TEMPERATURES

The oven temperatures in this book are for conventional ovens; if you have a fan-forced oven, decrease the temperature by 10–20 degrees.

	°C (Celsius)	°F (Fahrenheit)
Very slow	120	250
Slow	150	300
Moderately slow	160	325
Moderate	180	350
Moderately hot	200	400
Hot	220	425
Very hot	240	475

INDEX

133

 Published in 2022 by Are Media Books, Australia, in association with The Wiggles. Are Media Books is a division of Are Media Pty Ltd.

ARE MEDIA

Chief Executive Officer Jane Huxley

ARE MEDIA BOOKS

Group Publisher Nicole Byers

Editorial & Food Director
Sophia Young

Creative Director Hannah Blackmore

Managing Editor Stephanie Kistner

Art Director & Designer
Jeannel Cunanan

Senior Designer Kelsie Walker

Food Editor Domenica Reddie

Senior Editor Chantal Gibbs

Head of Operations David Scotto

Recipe Development Clare Maguire,
Domenica Reddie, Olivia Blackmore,
Elizabeth Fiducia, Laura Jenkins

Photographer James Moffatt

Stylist Olivia Blackmore

Photochef Clare Maguire,
Amanda Chebatte (party cakes)

Assistant Photochef Caitlyn McGrath

Published by Are Media Books,
a division of Are Media Pty Ltd,
54 Park St, Sydney; GPO Box 4088,
Sydney, NSW 2001, Australia
Ph +61 2 9282 8000
www.aremediabooks.com.au

© 2022 The Wiggles Pty Limited.
Manufactured by Are Media Pty
Limited under licence by The Wiggles.

www.thewiggles.com

A catalogue record for this
book is available from the
National Library of Australia.
ISBN 978-1-92586-668-1

Printed in China by
Leo Paper Products Ltd

International rights enquiries
internationalrights@aremedia.com.au

Order books
phone 1300 322 007 (within Australia)
or order online at
www.aremediabooks.com.au

Send recipe enquiries to
recipeenquiries@aremedia.com.au

**The publisher would like
to thank their models**
Rose Jhoty, Abigail Netto,
Mia Newbold, Heeva Patel,
Oliver Scotto, Thea Scotto,
Harvey Smith, Seraphia Tisi